Challenges of the Middle Class

C. P. Kumar
Reiki Healer
Roorkee - 247667, India

Disclaimer

While every effort has been made to ensure the accuracy and completeness of the content in this book, the author cannot guarantee that the information contained herein is error-free, up-to-date, or suitable for every individual circumstance.

The author shall not be held liable or responsible for any errors or omissions in the content of the book, nor for any damages, or losses that may arise from any actions taken based upon the suggestions or contents presented in the book.

Readers are advised to use their own judgment and discretion in applying the information provided in this book, and to consult with qualified professionals before taking any action based on the contents of this book. The author disclaims any and all liability or responsibility for any actions taken or not taken based on the information contained in this book.

DEDICATION

To the resilient and ever-adaptive members of the middle class, whose tenacity and determination inspire us to confront the multifaceted challenges of our time. Your pursuit of prosperity, work-life balance, and social justice embodies the aspirations of countless individuals around the world. This book is dedicated to you, the heart and soul of our societies, as you navigate the complexities of modern life with courage and grace. May the insights within these pages shed light on the path forward, igniting a brighter future for the middle class.

C. P. Kumar

CONTENTS

PREFACE

In the intricate tapestry of modern society, there exists a group that serves as both a foundation and a fulcrum. This group is the Middle Class – an ever-evolving, multifaceted, and diverse segment that constitutes the heart and soul of our communities. They are the teachers, the nurses, the engineers, the small business owners, the office workers, and the everyday heroes who form the backbone of our social fabric.

But what does it truly mean to be a member of the Middle Class? Why is this group so integral to the functioning of our world, and what challenges do they face as they navigate the complexities of contemporary life? This book delves deep into the heart of these questions, shedding light on the myriad challenges that the Middle Class grapples with daily.

Challenges of the Middle Class is a comprehensive exploration of the experiences, concerns, and aspirations of this vital social group. In its pages, we journey through a landscape of topics that encompass the very essence of the Middle Class experience. From economic pressures and educational hurdles to healthcare dilemmas, housing quandaries, and the intricate dance of work and family life – every chapter offers a lens through which we can view the struggles, triumphs, and enduring aspirations of the Middle Class.

The Middle Class has long been the linchpin of societal progress, but the strains they face are often understated or overlooked. This book seeks to change that, as it aims to both illuminate and inspire. In each chapter, we will dissect a specific facet of Middle Class life, shedding light on the realities they confront, and uncovering the potential pathways to a brighter future.

As you delve into the chapters that follow, you will traverse the intricate web of economic challenges, educational aspirations, and healthcare quandaries that define the Middle Class existence. You will witness the extraordinary resilience of individuals navigating dual-income households, parental responsibilities, and the ever-present specter of retirement planning.

Furthermore, the pages of this book will introduce you to the societal issues of our time that have a profound impact on the Middle Class: technological disruption, environmental concerns, social justice, and political engagement. It is our sincere hope that these pages will encourage open dialogue, prompt thoughtful reflection, and ultimately contribute to the collective well-being of this pivotal segment of society.

Throughout these pages, we present not only the obstacles but also the potential for growth, transformation, and resilience that the Middle Class embodies. We explore their role in shaping the world around them and how their actions have the power to influence policies, societal norms, and the path of future generations.

At its core, Challenges of the Middle Class is a clarion call for understanding, empathy, and change. It is a testament to the profound significance of the Middle Class in our society, and a recognition of the burdens they carry, the dreams they harbor, and the resilience that drives them forward.

As we embark on this journey through the lives and struggles of the Middle Class, let us remember that their challenges are not theirs alone; they are the challenges of society as a whole. Their resilience, their aspirations, and their stories are an integral part of the human experience, and they hold the keys to a more equitable, prosperous, and harmonious future.

Join us as we uncover the "Challenges of the Middle Class" and explore the path to a brighter tomorrow.

C. P. Kumar
Reiki Healer
Former Scientist 'G', National Institute of Hydrology
Roorkee - 247667, India
Web: https://www.angelfire.com/nh/cpkumar/virgo.html

The middle class, often considered the backbone of society, faces an array of challenges that are rapidly transforming the fabric of our social, economic, and political landscapes. These challenges are not only critical for the well-being of the middle class but also have profound implications for the overall stability and progress of nations. As we embark on this journey to explore the multifaceted challenges of the middle class, it is imperative to begin by delving into the very essence of who the middle class is, why they are pivotal, and how they have evolved over time.

Defining the Middle Class: Who Are They and Why Are They Important?

To embark on a meaningful exploration of the challenges facing the middle class, it is essential to define who they are and understand their significance in the broader context of society. The middle class, in a general sense, represents the economic and social stratum that falls between the lower-income and upper-income brackets. This segment of society is often characterized by moderate to comfortable incomes, access to education, and a certain degree of financial security.

The middle class forms the bridge between the economically disadvantaged and the affluent. They are instrumental in driving economic growth, maintaining social stability, and playing a significant role in the political dynamics of a nation. Understanding the middle class is imperative because their well-being and aspirations are closely tied to the overall health of a society.

Firstly, the middle class is the engine of economic growth. Their spending power fuels consumer markets, stimulates production, and creates jobs. This group represents a significant portion of the workforce, contributing to innovation, entrepreneurship, and the development of new technologies. Their capacity to invest in education and property fuels the demand for these industries, which, in turn, contributes to the growth of nations.

Secondly, the middle class serves as a bastion of social stability. When the middle class thrives, crime rates tend to be lower, and social unrest is less likely. The stability they provide acts as a buffer against radical political movements, ensuring a more balanced and inclusive political landscape.

Furthermore, the middle class plays an indispensable role in the democratic process. They are the driving force behind civil society, advocating for human rights, social justice, and political accountability. A strong middle class can act as a counterbalance to concentrated power and vested interests.

Historical Context: Evolution of the Middle Class and Its Societal Role

The middle class, as we understand it today, has a fascinating historical evolution. To grasp their role and challenges, it is essential to take a glimpse into their historical development.

The Emergence of the Middle Class: The Industrial Revolution of the late 18th and early 19th centuries marked the birth of the modern middle class. As industrialization transformed economies, people shifted from agrarian societies to urban centers, giving rise to a new class of professionals, entrepreneurs, and skilled workers. This transformative period redefined social structures, as people found new opportunities in the burgeoning industrial and commercial sectors.

The Rise of Consumer Culture: **The middle class's role in society was closely tied to the emergence of consumer culture. The ability to earn a living wage allowed them to participate in the market economy as both consumers and producers. This newfound economic power fueled the growth of cities, the development of new industries, and the expansion of education and culture.**

The Middle Class and Political Change: **The middle class played a significant role in shaping political ideologies and movements. They were at the forefront of calls for democratic reforms, human rights, and social justice. The revolutions of the 19th and 20th centuries, such as the French Revolution, were driven in part by the aspirations of the middle class for greater political influence.**

The Mid-20th Century Boom: **The post-World War II era witnessed the golden age of the middle class in many developed countries. Economic growth, government investments in education and healthcare, and strong labor unions created a robust middle class that enjoyed rising incomes, job security, and upward mobility. This period saw the construction of the "American Dream" and similar ideals in other nations. The *American Dream* is the belief that anyone, regardless of their background, can achieve success and prosperity through hard work and determination in the United States.**

Contemporary Challenges: **While the middle class has come a long way in its historical journey, the 21st century presents a fresh set of challenges. Economic inequality,** automation, globalization, and technological disruptions have threatened the middle-class way of life in many parts of the world. The cost of education and healthcare, housing affordability, and job insecurity have created a sense of anxiety and insecurity among the middle class.

Global Perspectives: It is important to note that the middle class is not a phenomenon confined to Western societies. In fact, emerging economies like China and India have witnessed a substantial rise in their middle class, altering global economic and political dynamics. Understanding the challenges faced by the middle class requires a global perspective.

Conclusion

The challenges facing the middle class are not isolated issues but are intricately intertwined with the broader social, economic, and political landscapes. The middle class's importance in shaping these landscapes, both historically and in the present, cannot be overstated. As the middle class grapples with economic pressures, job insecurity, and the ever-changing nature of work in the 21st century, it is vital to recognize the implications these challenges have for society as a whole.

This journey to explore the challenges of the middle class will take us through the multifaceted aspects of their lives – from economic pressures and the quest for financial security to their role in fostering social stability, political change, and advocating for human rights. Ultimately, this exploration seeks to shed light on the pivotal role of the middle class in the grand narrative of society, their historical evolution, and the critical challenges they face in the modern era.

In the subsequent chapters of this book, we will delve deeper into the specific challenges faced by the middle class and the potential solutions to address them. Through an informed understanding of their struggles, we can work towards a more inclusive, equitable, and prosperous society that benefits all its members, from the working class to the affluent, and recognizes the central role played by the middle class in shaping the world we live in.

Introduction

The middle class, often regarded as the backbone of any thriving economy, is currently facing unprecedented economic pressures. The very essence of the middle class lifestyle, with its stability, financial security, and upward mobility, is under threat. In this article, we will delve into the core issues that are squeezing the middle class. From stagnant wages to employment instability, these challenges are significantly impacting the lives of countless individuals and families, casting a shadow on their economic well-being.

Stagnant Wages: Coping with Rising Costs of Living

One of the most glaring economic pressures confronting the middle class is stagnant wages. For decades, the middle class has been the engine of economic growth, driving consumer spending and economic stability. However, wages have remained largely flat, failing to keep pace with the ever-increasing costs of living. This situation is primarily attributed to a multitude of factors, including globalization, automation, and changing labor dynamics.

1. The Great Wage Stagnation

Wage stagnation is not a new phenomenon, but it has become more pronounced in recent years. As the global economy has become increasingly interconnected, outsourcing and automation have become more prevalent. This has placed downward pressure on wages, as companies seek cost-effective ways to remain competitive. The result is that many middle-class workers find themselves stuck with salaries that haven't significantly increased in years, despite working harder and longer.

2. Cost of Living vs. Income

While wages have remained stagnant, the cost of living has soared. Housing, healthcare, education, and even groceries have become increasingly expensive. The middle class is left grappling with the challenge of stretching their income to cover these rising expenses. Many are finding it difficult to save for retirement, invest in their children's education, or purchase a home.

3. The Debt Trap

To cope with the disparity between income and expenses, many middle-class individuals have turned to credit. Credit cards, loans, and personal debt have become a means of survival for countless families. Unfortunately, this reliance on credit can lead to a dangerous cycle of debt, where individuals are unable to break free from the financial burdens they've accumulated.

4. Impact on Lifestyle

Stagnant wages have forced the middle class to reevaluate their lifestyles. The pursuit of a comfortable life characterized by homeownership, vacations, and savings for the future is increasingly elusive. Many are delaying major life events such as starting a family or retirement simply because they lack the financial stability they once expected.

Employment Instability: Navigating the Gig Economy and Job Insecurity

The traditional employment landscape has shifted significantly in recent years. The emergence of the gig economy and the prevalence of job insecurity have become central economic pressures facing the middle class. These challenges have transformed the nature of work, leaving many middle-class workers grappling with uncertainty and instability.

1. The Rise of the Gig Economy

The gig economy, typified by platforms like Uber, Airbnb, and freelancing, has redefined how people work. *Uber* is a transportation network company that provides on-demand ridesharing and transportation services through a mobile app, connecting passengers with drivers using their own vehicles. *Airbnb* is an online platform that allows people to rent or lease short-term lodging accommodations in private residences, offering a wide range of options for travelers and property owners. *Freelancing* is a work arrangement where individuals offer their skills and services on a project-by-project basis to various clients or companies, typically as independent contractors rather than full-time employees.

While it offers flexibility and opportunities, it also lacks many of the protections and benefits that traditional employment provides. Middle-class individuals are drawn to the gig economy as a way to supplement their income, but it often fails to offer the stability and security that full-time employment does.

2. Job Insecurity

Job insecurity is another major economic pressure faced by the middle class. Full-time, long-term employment with benefits has become increasingly rare. Many middle-class workers find themselves in precarious positions, with temporary contracts, irregular hours, and minimal job security. The fear of sudden job loss and the loss of employer-provided benefits is a constant source of anxiety for many.

3. The Erosion of Retirement Benefits

One significant casualty of employment instability is retirement security. In the United States, traditional pension plans have largely been replaced by 401(k) accounts, placing the onus of retirement planning squarely on the shoulders of individuals. This shift has left many middle-class workers uncertain about their financial future, especially in a volatile economy.

4. The Impact on Mental Health

The psychological toll of job insecurity and gig work is profound. Anxiety and stress are common experiences for middle-class workers who are unsure about their employment prospects. The gig economy, in particular, can be isolating and lead to feelings of instability and insecurity.

Conclusion

The economic pressures facing the middle class are multifaceted and challenging. Stagnant wages, coupled with the rising cost of living, have made it increasingly difficult for middle-class individuals and families to maintain the quality of life they aspire to. Employment instability, whether in the gig economy or due to job insecurity, adds another layer of uncertainty and stress.

Addressing these challenges is essential for the economic well-being and stability of the middle class, and by extension, the broader economy. Policy changes, improved worker protections, and a reevaluation of economic structures are necessary to ensure that the middle class can thrive and continue to be the engine of economic growth.

As we move forward, recognizing and addressing these economic pressures must be a priority for governments, employers, and individuals alike. The middle class is not only the heart of the economy but also a representation of social stability. Fostering economic security and stability for the middle class is crucial for ensuring a prosperous future for all.

Introduction

Education is often hailed as the great equalizer, a gateway to prosperity, and the means to break the cycle of poverty. However, in recent years, it has become increasingly apparent that the cost of education has escalated to a point where it poses significant challenges for the middle-class population. In this article, we will delve into the multifaceted challenges faced by the middle class regarding education, with a particular focus on the rising costs of education and the growing burden of student loan debt.

Rising Education Costs: Struggles to Afford Quality Education

One of the most pressing challenges that the middle class faces today is the soaring cost of education. Be it K-12 schooling (kindergarten through 12th grade) or higher education, the expense of securing a quality education has risen exponentially. Here, we'll explore various aspects of this issue.

1. The Skyrocketing Cost of Higher Education

In the United States and many other countries, the cost of higher education has reached staggering levels. Tuition fees, accommodation, and textbooks have become formidable financial burdens for middle-class families. Even with diligent saving, it can be challenging to accumulate the necessary funds for a college education.

The impact of these high costs is significant. Many students and their families face difficult choices, such as forgoing higher education altogether or settling for less prestigious institutions to save money.

2. Hidden Costs of Education

The cost of education extends beyond tuition fees and books. It encompasses transportation, living expenses, and extracurricular activities. These additional expenses can put a considerable strain on middle-class families, as they struggle to provide their children with a well-rounded educational experience.

3. Financial Aid Challenges

While scholarships and financial aid are available, they often come with strict eligibility criteria and a competitive application process. Middle-class families sometimes find themselves in the unfortunate middle ground – they don't qualify for substantial financial aid, yet they can't comfortably cover the costs without assistance.

4. Housing and School Districts

In many regions, the quality of education is closely tied to the neighborhood and the school district. To ensure their children receive a quality education, middle-class families may need to invest in more expensive housing, which can lead to financial strain.

5. Inequality in K-12 Education

Even before college, middle-class students face inequality in the K-12 education system. Public schools are often funded through property taxes, which means that students in affluent neighborhoods have access to better resources and educational opportunities. Middle-class families in less affluent areas can struggle to provide their children with the same advantages.

Student Loan Debt: Impact on Long-Term Financial Stability

As the middle class grapples with the rising costs of education, many are forced to turn to student loans to bridge the financial gap. However, the burden of student loan debt carries its own set of challenges and implications for long-term financial stability.

1. Accumulating Student Loan Debt

The middle class, unable to cover the full costs of education, increasingly relies on student loans. These loans may cover tuition, accommodation, and living expenses, but they come with a catch – interest. This interest can accumulate rapidly, turning a manageable loan into a substantial financial burden.

2. Post-Graduation Repayment Challenges

Once students graduate, the reality of repaying their student loans sets in. Middle-class graduates often find themselves allocating a significant portion of their monthly income to loan repayments, making it harder to save for the future or meet other financial goals. This can have long-term implications for financial stability.

3. Delayed Milestones

With a substantial student loan burden, middle-class individuals may find themselves delaying life milestones such as buying a home, starting a family, or saving for retirement. The burden of debt can stifle their ability to achieve these goals, leading to feelings of financial insecurity.

4. Psychological Toll

The psychological toll of student loan debt cannot be overstated. Middle-class individuals may experience anxiety, stress, and depression as they grapple with the responsibility of repaying their loans. This not only affects their financial well-being but also their overall quality of life.

5. Economic Impact on Society

The collective impact of student loan debt on the middle class can be detrimental to the broader economy. When a significant portion of the population is saddled with debt, they are less likely to invest, spend, and contribute to economic growth. This, in turn, can lead to a slowdown in economic activity.

6. Policy Challenges

Addressing the issue of student loan debt is not straightforward. Policymakers face challenges in striking a balance between providing access to education and ensuring that graduates are not overwhelmed by debt. Finding sustainable solutions to this problem is a complex undertaking.

Conclusion

Education is a cornerstone of personal and societal growth. It is a means of empowerment and advancement, a tool that allows individuals to reach their full potential and contribute meaningfully to society. However, as the cost of education continues to rise, the middle class faces unprecedented challenges in providing quality education for their children and pursuing higher education themselves.

The soaring costs of higher education, coupled with the burden of student loan debt, have created a perfect storm for middle-class individuals and families. They find themselves navigating a complex maze of financial choices, often at the expense of their long-term financial stability and well-being.

To address these challenges, there is a need for comprehensive solutions. This includes reevaluating the cost structure of education, exploring options for more affordable higher education, reforming student loan programs, and implementing policies that alleviate the financial burden on the middle class. Moreover, society must recognize the intrinsic value of accessible education and strive to create an environment where individuals can pursue learning without compromising their economic future.

In the end, education should be a beacon of hope, an avenue for personal growth, and a ladder to socioeconomic mobility, regardless of one's social or economic background. It is imperative that we work collectively to ensure that the challenges posed by the cost of education and student loan debt do not hinder the middle class from realizing their full potential and contributing to a brighter future for all.

Introduction

In an era characterized by profound socio-economic transformations and shifting demographics, the middle class finds itself grappling with a multitude of challenges. Among these challenges, healthcare stands out as a critical issue, and it is one that deeply affects the well-being of individuals and families. Access to quality healthcare, the affordability of medical services, the burden of insurance coverage, and the stigma surrounding mental health are all prominent concerns for the middle class. This article delves into these healthcare-related challenges, exploring the intricate balance between medical expenses and insurance coverage, the growing importance of mental health awareness, and the overall impact on the middle-class population.

Healthcare Affordability: Balancing Medical Expenses and Insurance Coverage

The middle class, often defined as those who fall between the lower and upper income brackets, represents a significant portion of the population in many countries. They play a pivotal role in the economy, and their well-being is crucial for societal stability. However, when it comes to healthcare, the middle class often finds itself walking a tightrope between the need for quality medical services and the financial burden associated with them.

1. Rising Medical Costs

The cost of healthcare has been steadily rising, and middle-class families are feeling the strain. The expenses associated with doctor visits, hospital stays, medications, and medical procedures have become exorbitant in many countries. Middle-class individuals often find themselves in a precarious financial situation when they or their family members require medical attention.

2. Insurance Coverage Dilemma

To mitigate the impact of high medical expenses, many people turn to health insurance. While insurance can be a lifeline in times of medical need, it's not always affordable or comprehensive. Middle-class families often face the challenge of choosing insurance plans that balance coverage and cost. They need coverage that protects them from financial catastrophe while still being within their budget.

3. Balancing Act

The middle class must navigate the complex terrain of deductibles, co-pays, premiums, and out-of-pocket maximums when selecting insurance. They must weigh the financial burden of monthly premiums against the potential cost of medical services. Striking the right balance between insurance coverage and out-of-pocket expenses is a constant challenge, one that can have far-reaching financial consequences.

4. Unforeseen Medical Emergencies

One of the greatest fears for middle-class families is the unexpected medical emergency. When such events occur, they can disrupt financial stability and jeopardize the family's future. A sudden illness, injury, or the diagnosis of a chronic condition can strain finances and lead to difficult choices, such as delaying essential medical care or going into debt to cover expenses.

The middle class isn't a homogeneous group, and disparities within this segment are prevalent. Some middle-class individuals may have better access to healthcare due to their financial standing, while others struggle to afford even basic medical services. This disparity can be attributed to income variations within the middle class and regional disparities in healthcare accessibility.

Mental Health Awareness: Addressing the Stigma and Challenges

While physical health is an essential aspect of healthcare, the middle class also faces significant challenges related to mental health. The stigma associated with mental health issues, along with barriers to access and affordability, creates a perfect storm of difficulties for middle-class individuals and families.

1. Stigma Surrounding Mental Health

Stigma is a formidable obstacle to mental health awareness and treatment. In many societies, seeking help for mental health issues is viewed with prejudice and shame. This stigma often prevents middle-class individuals from seeking the support they need, exacerbating mental health problems and leading to delayed or inadequate treatment.

2. Lack of Access to Mental Health Services

Mental health services are not as readily available or affordable as physical health services. Middle-class individuals may struggle to find qualified mental health professionals, and even when they do, the cost of therapy or psychiatric care can be prohibitive. This limited access to mental health services further hinders their ability to address psychological challenges.

3. The Balancing Act: Mental Health and Work

Middle-class individuals often face immense pressure in their professional lives. The stress of maintaining a job, balancing work and family responsibilities, and the demands of modern life can take a toll on mental health. However, taking time off work for mental health reasons may come with the fear of job insecurity or lost income, creating a dilemma that can worsen mental health concerns.

4. Impact on Family Dynamics

Mental health issues don't affect only the individual; they can also strain family dynamics. Middle-class families may find it challenging to address mental health concerns within the family, leading to increased stress and disrupted relationships. The stigma surrounding mental health makes it difficult for families to communicate openly about these issues and seek the necessary support.

5. The Economic Burden

Mental health problems can result in lost productivity at work, increased medical expenses, and the need for ongoing treatment. The financial strain caused by mental health issues can push middle-class families further towards financial instability, adding another layer of complexity to their healthcare challenges.

Conclusion

In navigating the labyrinth of healthcare, the middle class faces formidable challenges. The rising costs of medical services, the complex landscape of insurance coverage, and the fear of unexpected medical emergencies loom as constant threats to financial stability. Additionally, the stigma surrounding mental health, combined with limited access to mental health services, adds to the burden of middle-class individuals and families. As we acknowledge and address these issues, it is essential to work towards solutions that can alleviate the healthcare challenges faced by the middle class.

To address the affordability of healthcare, governments and healthcare providers should strive to implement policies and practices that make medical services more accessible and affordable. This includes measures to control rising healthcare costs, provide subsidies for insurance coverage, and develop innovative models of healthcare delivery that prioritize cost-effectiveness without compromising quality.

In the realm of mental health, raising awareness and eliminating the stigma are paramount. Public education campaigns should emphasize the importance of seeking help for mental health issues and provide resources for those in need. Additionally, governments and healthcare systems must invest in expanding access to mental health services and ensuring they are affordable for all, regardless of socio-economic status.

Ultimately, addressing healthcare challenges for the middle class is not just a matter of policy; it is a societal responsibility. The well-being of the middle class is inextricably linked to the overall health of a nation's economy and society. By recognizing the unique struggles of the middle class and implementing comprehensive solutions, we can help ensure that access to quality healthcare is a fundamental right, rather than an unattainable dream. In doing so, we can create a more equitable and healthier society for all.

Introduction

Housing is a fundamental aspect of our lives, and it plays a significant role in defining our standard of living. For the middle class, securing a comfortable and affordable place to call home can be a daunting task in today's world. This article delves into the challenges faced by the middle class when it comes to housing, with a focus on housing affordability and urbanization pressures.

Housing Affordability: Dealing with High Rents and Unattainable Mortgages

The dream of homeownership is deeply ingrained in the psyche of the middle class. Owning a home represents stability, security, and a sense of accomplishment. However, the rising costs of housing have made this dream increasingly challenging to attain.

1. Soaring House Prices

The steep increase in housing prices, especially in major cities, has made purchasing a home an uphill battle for the middle class. Escalating demand, limited housing supply, and real estate speculation have contributed to skyrocketing house prices. Middle-class families are often caught in a Catch-22 situation where the longer they wait to buy a home, the further out of reach it becomes.

2. High Rent Burden

For those unable to buy a home, renting becomes the only option. However, high rents can place a significant burden on middle-class households. A substantial portion of their income is earmarked for rent, leaving little room for savings and other essential expenses.

3. Access to Mortgages

A mortgage is a loan provided by a financial institution, typically a bank, that enables individuals to purchase real estate by using the property as collateral for the loan, with repayment occurring over a specified period of time. Securing a mortgage to buy a home is another obstacle for the middle class. The stringent lending criteria, large down payment requirements, and high-interest rates can deter many potential homeowners. While low-interest rates may seem attractive, they often come with stricter credit score requirements, making it difficult for middle-class individuals with average credit scores to qualify.

4. Financial Insecurity

Housing affordability issues have a ripple effect on the overall financial security of middle-class families. The high costs of housing can lead to a lack of disposable income, making it challenging to save for the future, invest, or meet other financial goals. Many middle-class families find themselves living paycheck to paycheck, with little financial cushion.

5. Gentrification

Gentrification is the process in which wealthier individuals and businesses move into a previously disadvantaged or deteriorated neighborhood, often leading to the displacement of low-income residents and changes in the area's character and affordability. Gentrification has a profound impact on housing affordability. As neighborhoods are revitalized, property values rise, often pushing out long-time middle-class residents who can no longer afford to live there. This process can result in the displacement of communities and a loss of the sense of belonging.

Urbanization Pressures: Finding Suitable Housing in Crowded Cities

Urbanization is an undeniable global trend, with people flocking to cities for better employment opportunities and improved quality of life. However, the influx of residents into urban areas has created housing challenges for the middle class, as they compete for limited resources and face the consequences of urban sprawl.

1. Limited Space and Increased Competition

Urban areas, particularly in megacities, face limited available land for housing. The increasing population density and competition for housing options often lead to inflated prices and a lack of affordable housing units. Middle-class individuals and families must compete with a growing number of prospective tenants or buyers, which further drives up costs.

2. Commuting Woes

As housing within city centers becomes prohibitively expensive, middle-class individuals often find themselves forced to live in the suburbs or distant areas. This results in long and stressful commutes, impacting both their quality of life and overall well-being. Longer commutes also mean additional expenses and contribute to traffic congestion and environmental issues.

3. Infrastructure Strain

Rapid urbanization places immense strain on city infrastructure, including public transportation, roads, and utilities. Overcrowded cities can lead to inadequate public services and deteriorating living conditions. This affects the middle class, who rely on these services for their daily lives.

4. Quality of Life

Urbanization pressures can diminish the overall quality of life for the middle class. Noise pollution, lack of green spaces, and limited access to amenities can negatively impact mental and physical health. The middle class often struggles to balance the allure of urban living with the realities of day-to-day existence in overcrowded cities.

5. Alternative Housing Solutions

In response to these challenges, some middle-class individuals have explored alternative housing solutions. Co-living, micro-apartments, and shared housing arrangements have gained popularity as ways to mitigate the high costs of living in cities. These solutions may provide affordability and community, but they also raise questions about privacy and long-term sustainability.

Conclusion

Housing is a vital aspect of middle-class life, but it is plagued by numerous challenges, primarily related to affordability and urbanization pressures. The dream of homeownership remains elusive for many due to soaring house prices, high rents, and limited access to mortgages. The financial instability resulting from these issues can hinder the middle class's ability to save and invest in their future.

Urbanization has created a scenario where the middle class must compete for limited housing options and often contend with long commutes and overcrowded city infrastructure. The strain on quality of life and the environment poses additional challenges.

To address these housing challenges, policymakers, urban planners, and developers must work together to create affordable housing options, improve transportation infrastructure, and foster sustainable urban growth. The middle class deserves the opportunity to enjoy the benefits of homeownership and urban living without being burdened by financial insecurity and poor living conditions.

In the face of these challenges, it is essential to recognize the resilience and adaptability of the middle class. They continue to seek innovative housing solutions and advocate for policies that promote affordable and sustainable living in the cities they call home. As we move forward, it is crucial to support and empower the middle class in their pursuit of secure and comfortable housing.

Introduction

The concept of work-life balance has become an increasingly prevalent topic in the modern world, particularly for middle-class families. As the demands of the workplace continue to evolve, and as societal norms shift, many families find themselves navigating the often tricky terrain of managing careers while also nurturing a fulfilling family life. This article explores the challenges faced by middle-class families as they strive to maintain equilibrium between their professional responsibilities and family commitments. We delve into the dynamics of dual-income households, the significance of parental leave and childcare, and ultimately, the pursuit of a harmonious work-life balance.

Dual-Income Households: Juggling Careers and Family Life

The dynamics of the modern family have changed dramatically over the past few decades. Dual-income households have become the new norm in many middle-class families, with both parents pursuing careers to maintain financial stability and meet their aspirations. This shift brings with it both advantages and challenges.

1. Economic Stability and Ambitions

One of the primary motivations behind dual-income households is the pursuit of economic stability and, in many cases, upward mobility. Middle-class families often rely on two incomes to afford the essentials like housing, education, and healthcare. The desire to provide children with a better future and access to opportunities motivates parents to invest in their careers. However, the pursuit of economic stability and ambitious career goals can sometimes lead to a lack of quality time spent with family.

2. Time Management Challenges

Balancing two careers and a family can be a significant challenge. Parents must juggle their work schedules, meetings, and deadlines with school pickups, soccer practices, and family dinners. The middle-class ethos of 'having it all' sometimes places unrealistic expectations on parents, leading to feelings of stress and exhaustion.

3. Communication and Support

Effective communication is crucial in dual-income households. Sharing household responsibilities, discussing work commitments, and scheduling quality family time are essential for maintaining a harmonious family life. Middle-class families often rely on support networks, including extended family members and close friends, to help manage their demanding schedules.

4. Gender Roles and Expectations

The evolving nature of dual-income households also challenges traditional gender roles and expectations. Both parents are active contributors to the workforce, and the allocation of household responsibilities is becoming more gender-neutral. However, navigating these shifts can sometimes be a source of tension and conflict, as it requires a reevaluation of traditional family roles.

Parental Leave and Childcare: Striving for Work-Life Balance

Parental leave and childcare play a pivotal role in middle-class families' pursuit of work-life balance. These aspects are not only a matter of personal choice but are also influenced by societal norms and government policies.

1. Parental Leave

Parental leave policies vary significantly from one country to another. In middle-class families, the availability and duration of parental leave can significantly impact the ability to balance work and family life. While some countries provide generous paid leave options, others offer limited or no support.

2. Balancing Career and Childcare

One of the dilemmas faced by middle-class parents is the decision of when to return to work after childbirth. Many parents grapple with the choice between advancing their careers and providing hands-on care to their children during the critical early years. This decision can affect their career trajectories and long-term financial stability.

3. Childcare Options

Middle-class families often have access to a variety of childcare options, such as daycare centers, nannies (individuals employed to provide childcare and perform various domestic tasks within a household, often on a live-in or live-out basis, to support working parents or guardians in the care of their children), or family members. Choosing the right form of childcare involves assessing factors like cost, convenience, and the quality of care provided. These decisions can have a significant impact on work-life balance.

Workplace policies and culture also influence how parents balance work and family life. Employers that provide flexibility, such as remote work options and flexible hours, can be instrumental in helping middle-class parents navigate their dual roles. In contrast, employers with rigid structures may inadvertently hinder work-life balance.

Conclusion

Balancing work and family life is an ongoing challenge for middle-class families. The dynamics of dual-income households and the complexities of parental leave and childcare decisions require careful consideration and constant adaptation. Achieving work-life balance is not a one-size-fits-all endeavor; it varies from family to family based on their unique circumstances, goals, and available resources.

Ultimately, middle-class families need to prioritize communication, support, and flexibility to navigate the delicate balance between their professional and family lives. Society, in turn, can support this endeavor through policies that promote gender equality, parental leave, and accessible, high-quality childcare. As the concept of family and work balance continues to evolve, middle-class families must continue to adapt and strive for a life that is both professionally and personally fulfilling.

Introduction

Retirement planning is an essential yet often overlooked aspect of financial stability for the middle class. In today's dynamic economic landscape, where pension uncertainties loom and the cost of elderly care is rising, middle-class individuals find themselves facing unique challenges when it comes to securing a comfortable retirement. This article explores the intricacies of retirement planning for the middle class, shedding light on how individuals can navigate the complexities and uncertainties of this critical life phase.

Pension Uncertainties: Navigating Retirement Savings in Changing Economic Landscapes

Pensions have traditionally been a reliable source of income for retirees, but their stability is now being questioned in the face of changing economic realities. In an era characterized by economic volatility and shifting job market dynamics, middle-class individuals must adapt their retirement planning strategies to address pension uncertainties effectively.

1. The Decline of Traditional Pensions

Traditional defined benefit pension plans, which guarantee a specific retirement income based on years of service and final salary, have become increasingly rare in the private sector. Instead, many employers have shifted to defined contribution plans, such as 401(k)s, where employees contribute a portion of their salary, and employers may match a certain percentage. While these plans offer more control and flexibility, they also transfer the investment and longevity risks to the employees.

Middle-class workers who relied on traditional pensions may need to rethink their retirement strategies. They must become savvier about managing their investments, assessing risk tolerance, and diversifying their portfolios to ensure they can generate sufficient income to maintain their desired lifestyle in retirement.

2. Social Security and Its Uncertainties

Social Security refers to a government program in the United States (and similar programs in other countries) that provides financial assistance, particularly retirement benefits, to eligible individuals based on their work history and contributions to the system. It also offers disability and survivor benefits.

Social Security is a lifeline for many middle-class retirees, providing a foundation of financial support. However, the program faces demographic challenges with the aging population and a decreasing worker-to-beneficiary ratio. To maintain the program's viability, policymakers may need to make adjustments, such as raising the retirement age, reducing benefits, or increasing payroll taxes.

Middle-class individuals need to consider these potential changes when planning for retirement. They should also explore strategies for optimizing their Social Security benefits, such as delaying claiming to receive higher monthly payments or coordinating benefits with a spouse.

For many middle-class workers, employer-sponsored retirement plans like 401(k)s play a significant role in their retirement savings. To navigate pension uncertainties, individuals should take full advantage of these opportunities. Maximize contributions, especially when employers offer matching contributions, and make informed investment choices based on long-term financial goals.

Additionally, regularly reviewing and adjusting retirement portfolios in response to market fluctuations is crucial. Seeking advice from financial advisors can be invaluable in ensuring that investments align with retirement objectives while managing risk.

Elderly Care: Balancing Financial Support for Aging Parents and Planning for One's Own Retirement

The middle class often faces a unique financial dilemma: the need to provide support for aging parents while simultaneously planning for their own retirement. This balancing act can be challenging, but it's a reality for many individuals in this demographic.

1. The Rising Cost of Elderly Care

The cost of elderly care has been steadily increasing, and it can put a significant strain on middle-class families. Expenses related to long-term care, medical bills, and home modifications can erode retirement savings if not planned for appropriately.

One strategy middle-class individuals can employ is long-term care insurance. This insurance can help cover the expenses associated with nursing homes, in-home care, or assisted living facilities. While it's an added expense, it can prevent the depletion of personal savings earmarked for retirement.

2. The Sandwich Generation

Middle-class individuals often find themselves in the "sandwich generation", meaning they are simultaneously caring for aging parents and supporting their own children. This dynamic can be financially and emotionally challenging. It's essential to set clear boundaries and expectations, both with aging parents and children, to ensure that the financial impact does not jeopardize retirement plans.

Additionally, individuals may need to explore alternative options for elderly care, such as community programs, government assistance, or shared responsibilities with siblings, to reduce the financial burden.

3. Estate Planning and Inheritance

When balancing financial support for aging parents and retirement planning, it's crucial to consider estate planning. A well-thought-out estate plan can help ensure that assets are distributed according to your wishes, minimizing potential conflicts among heirs and beneficiaries.

Furthermore, estate planning can help middle-class individuals safeguard their own retirement savings. By creating a clear plan for the distribution of assets, they can protect their financial well-being and their loved ones' future.

Conclusion

Navigating retirement planning challenges in the middle class requires a proactive and adaptable approach. As pension uncertainties persist, individuals must become more self-reliant in managing their retirement savings. Leveraging employer-sponsored retirement plans and optimizing Social Security benefits are crucial components of this strategy.

Simultaneously, middle-class individuals often find themselves juggling financial support for aging parents and their own retirement goals. By planning ahead, addressing the rising cost of elderly care, and considering long-term care insurance, they can strike a balance that safeguards their financial well-being.

Estate planning should not be neglected either, as it helps protect one's assets and ensures the smooth transition of wealth to the next generation. In summary, middle-class retirement planning necessitates a multifaceted approach that addresses pension uncertainties, the rising cost of elderly care, and the nuances of financial support. By taking a proactive stance and seeking professional advice when necessary, individuals in the middle class can better navigate these challenges and secure a comfortable retirement.

Introduction

In an ever-evolving global landscape, the middle class stands as a vital cornerstone of society. It's a social stratum that bridges the gap between the rich and the poor, fostering economic stability, social cohesion, and overall progress. However, the challenges facing the middle class are multifaceted and ever-present, and one of the most significant issues they encounter is social mobility. Social mobility, the capacity of individuals to rise or fall in socioeconomic status, is a critical aspect of a healthy society. This article delves into the concept of social mobility, focusing on its role in the middle class, with particular attention to the impact of education and the limitations and barriers that hinder this upward journey.

Education as an Equalizer: Analyzing the Role of Education in Upward Mobility

Education has long been heralded as the great equalizer, offering individuals a means to escape the confines of their birth circumstances and propel themselves upwards in society. For the middle class, education plays an indispensable role in achieving upward mobility.

The Power of Education: Education provides the knowledge and skills necessary to secure well-paying jobs and access better opportunities. It is the conduit through which individuals can overcome the economic hurdles that often shackle them to their current socio-economic status.

Access to Quality Education: A fundamental challenge in the quest for social mobility within the middle class is the accessibility to quality education. Disparities in educational quality exist, perpetuating inequality. Students in underprivileged areas often receive an education inferior in both resources and opportunities. The lack of access to quality education can stifle the potential of individuals and inhibit their upward mobility.

Student Debt: Another hurdle that many middle-class individuals face in their pursuit of education is the burden of student debt. The cost of higher education has risen significantly, creating a financial strain that affects graduates for years to come. Student debt not only impedes financial stability but can also hinder the ability to invest in future opportunities.

The Skills Mismatch: The middle class often experiences difficulty in translating their education into the right career path. The skills mismatch between the qualifications acquired and the demands of the job market can lead to underemployment or unemployment, inhibiting social mobility.

Limited Opportunities: Addressing the Glass Ceiling and Professional Advancement

Social mobility doesn't stop with education; professional advancement and career growth are equally crucial for middle-class individuals striving to reach a higher socio-economic status.

The Glass Ceiling: The glass ceiling, a metaphorical barrier that hinders women and minorities from advancing to top positions in their careers, is a significant challenge for social mobility. Breaking through this ceiling remains a complex issue, particularly for middle-class individuals who must combat both gender and socio-economic biases.

Income Inequality: The middle class often finds itself stuck in a cycle of income inequality. Wage stagnation and limited opportunities for career progression can make it challenging for individuals to achieve financial stability and, consequently, upward mobility.

Geographical Mobility: Mobility is not just about social or economic factors but also geographical ones. Opportunities are not uniformly distributed across regions, and the middle class may need to consider moving to access better prospects. This poses significant challenges for those with familial and social ties that anchor them in less advantageous locations.

Overwork and Burnout: The pressures of climbing the corporate ladder can lead to overwork and burnout, affecting both physical and mental health. These challenges can hinder middle-class individuals' progress and increase the risk of downward mobility due to health-related issues.

Conclusion

The challenges facing the middle class regarding social mobility are complex, multifaceted, and often interconnected. Education remains a fundamental driver of upward mobility, but it is hindered by issues such as disparities in access to quality education, student debt, and skills mismatches. Moreover, barriers like the glass ceiling, income inequality, geographical mobility, and overwork further complicate the journey towards social advancement.

Addressing these challenges necessitates a comprehensive approach, combining policies that enhance educational opportunities, improve income equality, and promote workplace diversity. Initiatives like reducing the cost of education, addressing the skills gap, and implementing flexible work arrangements can make a significant difference. Promoting mentorship and networking opportunities can also help individuals navigate the complexities of career advancement.

The middle class, as the backbone of society, deserves the chance to prosper and reach their full potential. Tackling these challenges of social mobility is not just a matter of economic equity; it's about creating a society where individuals have the freedom to pursue their aspirations and contribute to the greater good. By breaking down these barriers, we can strengthen the middle class and, in turn, build a more equitable and prosperous society for all.

Introduction

The middle class forms the backbone of many economies, providing stability and driving consumption. However, in the pursuit of financial stability, they often grapple with a series of challenges, one of which is debt management. The management of debt and financial resources is a pivotal aspect of middle-class life, as it influences financial security, lifestyle choices, and future opportunities. In this article, we will delve into the complexities of debt and financial management within the middle-class demographic, exploring issues like credit card debt, consumer debt implications, the importance of financial literacy, and strategies for responsible money management.

Credit Card Debt: Managing Consumer Debt and Its Implications

Credit cards are a ubiquitous part of modern life, offering convenience and flexibility in spending. However, they also pose a significant challenge for middle-class individuals and families when it comes to managing consumer debt.

1. Understanding the Allure of Credit Cards

Credit cards are often the first step into the world of debt for many middle-class individuals. The allure of instant gratification, rewards, and deferred payments can be enticing, but if not managed wisely, they can become a source of financial stress.

2. The Debt Spiral

One of the dangers of credit card debt is the ease with which it can accumulate. Minimum payments and revolving credit can trap individuals in a never-ending cycle of debt, with interest accruing at high rates. This spiral can make it challenging for middle-class families to achieve their financial goals, such as homeownership, education, or retirement savings.

3. Managing Credit Card Debt

To tackle credit card debt effectively, it's crucial to have a well-thought-out plan. This plan should include:

Setting a budget: **Create a realistic budget that outlines income, expenses, and debt repayment. This will help identify areas where cuts can be made to allocate more funds towards debt reduction.**

Reducing interest rates: **Explore options like balance transfers to lower interest rates, which can save money and expedite the debt payoff process.**

Avoiding impulse spending: **Middle-class individuals should exercise self-discipline and avoid unnecessary expenditures that can lead to further credit card debt.**

Snowball or avalanche method: **Snowball method is a debt repayment strategy that prioritizes paying off the smallest debts first, regardless of interest rates, to build momentum. Avalanche Method is a debt repayment strategy that focuses on paying off the debt with the highest interest rate first, potentially saving more money on interest over time. Consider these popular debt reduction strategies to pay off credit card balances effectively.**

Seeking professional help: If the debt situation becomes unmanageable, middle-class individuals should not hesitate to seek assistance from credit counseling agencies or financial advisors.

Financial Literacy: Promoting Responsible Money Management

One of the key pillars of effective debt and financial management is financial literacy. The middle class must understand the basics of personal finance to make informed decisions and navigate the complexities of the financial world.

1. The Importance of Financial Education

Financial literacy is not just a luxury; it is a necessity for everyone, regardless of income or social status. Middle-class individuals need to understand concepts like budgeting, saving, investing, and the impact of debt on their financial future.

2. Access to Financial Education

Middle-class individuals should have access to financial education through schools, community programs, and digital resources. Financial literacy programs can empower individuals to make sound financial decisions and avoid common pitfalls that lead to debt.

3. Budgeting and Saving

Middle-class families should learn to create and stick to a budget. Budgeting helps in tracking income and expenses, making it easier to save for future needs and manage debt more effectively.

4. Understanding Debt

An essential aspect of financial literacy is understanding the different types of debt and their implications. This includes understanding the differences between good debt (e.g., a mortgage) and bad debt (e.g., high-interest credit card debt).

5. Investing Wisely

Middle-class individuals should also have a basic understanding of investment options, such as stocks, bonds, and retirement accounts. This knowledge can help them grow their wealth over time and achieve long-term financial goals.

6. Emergency Funds

Financial literacy emphasizes the importance of building an emergency fund. Having savings set aside for unexpected expenses can prevent individuals from relying on credit cards to cover emergencies.

7. Debt Avoidance and Management

Financial literacy education should focus on helping middle-class individuals avoid unnecessary debt and manage existing debt wisely. This includes understanding the implications of late payments, high-interest rates, and the impact on credit scores.

The middle class should be encouraged to think about their long-term financial goals, such as homeownership, retirement, and education for their children. These goals can be achieved through prudent financial planning and management.

Conclusion

The challenges of the middle class in managing debt and financial resources are significant but not insurmountable. Credit card debt, with its allure and potential for a debt spiral, is a major concern for middle-class individuals. However, with proper planning, discipline, and seeking professional assistance when necessary, credit card debt can be effectively managed and reduced.

Moreover, financial literacy is a crucial tool in the middle-class arsenal for responsible money management. It equips individuals with the knowledge and skills needed to navigate the complex financial world, make informed decisions, and avoid common pitfalls that lead to debt. Financial education should be readily accessible to the middle class, enabling them to create budgets, save, invest wisely, and understand the implications of various types of debt.

In conclusion, the challenges of the middle class in managing debt and finances are a reflection of the broader economic landscape. However, with the right tools and knowledge, middle-class individuals can take control of their financial futures, achieve their goals, and secure their place in the ever-evolving economic world. By addressing credit card debt and promoting financial literacy, we can empower the middle class to make sound financial decisions, build wealth, and ultimately achieve financial stability.

Introduction

Technological disruption, driven by rapid advances in automation and digital technology, is reshaping the economic landscape, causing profound effects on the middle class. In an era of digital transformation, the middle class faces unprecedented challenges and opportunities, demanding adaptability and resilience. This article explores the multifaceted aspects of technological disruption and its impact on the middle class, emphasizing the need for skill adaptation and addressing the digital divide.

The Digital Revolution: A Disruptive Force

The advent of the digital age has ushered in a wave of unprecedented technological change. This revolution encompasses automation, artificial intelligence, the Internet of Things (IoT), and other innovations, fundamentally altering the way industries operate and redefining the skills and qualifications required to thrive in the job market.

Automation and Job Displacement: Adapting Skills to Match Changing Job Market Demands

1. The Displacement Dilemma

Automation has become a double-edged sword, promising increased efficiency and reduced costs for businesses but posing a direct threat to many traditional middle-class jobs. Routine and repetitive tasks are increasingly automated, affecting various sectors, from manufacturing to customer service.

2. Skills for the Future

To combat the risk of job displacement, middle-class workers must acquire skills that are less susceptible to automation. These include problem-solving, critical thinking, creativity, and emotional intelligence. Investing in education and continuous learning is vital for staying relevant in the job market.

3. The Upside of Automation

While automation poses challenges, it also presents opportunities. The automation of routine tasks can free up human workers to focus on more complex, creative, and value-added tasks. By embracing automation as a tool to enhance productivity, the middle class can benefit from its potential.

4. The Gig Economy

The gig economy has emerged as a response to technological disruption. Middle-class individuals can leverage their skills and talents to participate in the gig economy, offering freelance services and enjoying flexibility in their work arrangements.

Digital Divide: Access to Technology and Its Impact on Education and Employment

1. The Access Gap

The digital divide, characterized by unequal access to technology, remains a significant challenge for the middle class. Disparities in internet access, computer literacy, and digital infrastructure create obstacles in terms of education and employment opportunities.

2. Education and Online Learning

The pandemic accelerated the shift towards online education, highlighting the importance of equitable access to digital resources. The middle class must address this gap to ensure that all members can access quality education, regardless of their socioeconomic status.

3. Telecommuting and Remote Work

The rise of remote work has become a prominent feature of the digital revolution. While it offers flexibility, it also accentuates the digital divide. Those with limited access to technology may find themselves excluded from remote job opportunities, affecting their earning potential and job security.

4. Government Initiatives and Digital Inclusion

Governments and organizations are increasingly recognizing the importance of digital inclusion. Programs and policies aimed at reducing the digital divide, such as subsidizing internet access or providing free digital skills training, can help bridge the gap and empower the middle class.

Conclusion

Technological disruption is an ongoing force that continues to shape the middle class's destiny. In the face of automation, middle-class workers must adapt their skills to remain competitive in the job market. The emphasis should be on nurturing skills that are less susceptible to automation, such as critical thinking and creativity. By viewing automation as a tool rather than a threat, individuals can harness its potential to enhance their productivity.

Simultaneously, the digital divide poses a critical challenge. Unequal access to technology jeopardizes education and employment opportunities for those on the wrong side of the divide. It's imperative to address this gap through government initiatives, corporate responsibility, and community efforts to ensure that all members of the middle class have a fair chance to thrive in the digital age.

In conclusion, the challenges of the middle class in the face of technological disruption are significant but not insurmountable. Through continuous learning, adaptability, and a commitment to digital inclusion, the middle class can navigate these challenges, seize opportunities, and secure their place in the ever-evolving digital landscape. By doing so, they can not only survive but thrive in the digital era, contributing to a more inclusive and innovative society.

Introduction

In an era marked by unprecedented technological advancements and societal progress, the middle class finds itself grappling with a unique set of challenges that stem from their socio-economic position. Among these challenges, environmental concerns have emerged as a prominent and pressing issue, impacting the lives, choices, and aspirations of the middle class. In this article, we will delve into the multifaceted environmental concerns faced by the middle class and explore how these challenges are intertwined with the broader theme of sustainability. We will discuss the cost of sustainable living, the disproportionate impact of climate change on the middle class, and offer insights into how this segment of society can navigate these challenges.

Sustainable Living Costs: Balancing Eco-friendly Choices with Budget Constraints

Sustainability, though a worthy goal, is often seen as a privilege, as many eco-friendly options come with a premium price tag. The middle class, comprising individuals and families with moderate incomes, grapple with the challenging task of making eco-conscious choices while managing their budgets. Here, we examine the factors that make sustainable living a formidable challenge for the middle class.

Middle-class individuals often face the dilemma of choosing between affordability and eco-friendliness. It's no secret that green products, whether organic food, energy-efficient appliances, or electric vehicles, often come with a higher upfront cost. While the long-term benefits of such choices are evident, the initial investment can be a deterrent for middle-class families.

For example, electric cars are more energy-efficient and have a smaller carbon footprint compared to their gasoline counterparts. However, their higher purchase price and limited charging infrastructure make them less accessible to middle-class consumers. Similarly, organic food is healthier and has a lower environmental impact, but it tends to be more expensive than conventionally grown produce, making it less attainable for many middle-class households.

2. The Burden of Energy Efficiency Upgrades

Home energy efficiency is a critical component of sustainable living, but upgrading a home to be more energy-efficient can be costly. Middle-class homeowners often struggle to invest in energy-saving improvements like insulation, solar panels, or energy-efficient HVAC systems. These upgrades can yield long-term savings on utility bills and reduce carbon emissions, but they require a significant initial financial outlay.

3. Transportation Choices

Climate-conscious middle-class individuals may want to opt for public transportation or purchase hybrid or electric vehicles. However, public transportation systems are often underdeveloped in suburban areas where many middle-class families live, making car ownership a necessity. Moreover, electric or hybrid vehicles, while reducing the carbon footprint, can be more expensive than traditional gasoline-powered cars.

4. The Food Dilemma

Middle-class families are also concerned about the environmental impact of their food choices. They often seek to consume sustainably sourced, locally grown, and organic foods. However, the price disparity between conventional and organic products can be significant, making it difficult for middle-class households to make eco-friendly dietary choices without straining their budgets.

5. Balancing Short-term and Long-term Costs

In many cases, the middle class must weigh the immediate costs of eco-friendly choices against long-term benefits. For example, energy-efficient appliances are typically more expensive upfront, but they can lead to substantial savings on energy bills over time. Middle-class consumers must find a balance that aligns with their budgets and environmental values, which can be a complex juggling act.

Climate Change's Disproportionate Impact: How the Middle Class is Affected

The middle class not only grapples with the financial aspects of sustainable living but also faces the disproportionate impact of climate change. While climate change is a global issue, its consequences are not evenly distributed, and the middle class bears a unique burden.

1. Vulnerability to Extreme Weather Events

Climate change is intensifying extreme weather events such as hurricanes, droughts, and wildfires. Middle-class homeowners, particularly those in suburban or semi-urban areas, are susceptible to property damage and financial losses due to these events. While insurance may provide some relief, middle-class families often find themselves underinsured or facing high deductibles.

2. Health and Healthcare Costs

The middle class often faces increased healthcare costs related to climate change. Rising temperatures can lead to heat-related illnesses and exacerbate respiratory conditions. Middle-class families may find themselves spending more on healthcare to address climate-related health issues or protect themselves from exposure to pollutants.

3. Job Insecurity

Many middle-class individuals work in industries vulnerable to the impacts of climate change, such as agriculture, manufacturing, and construction. As extreme weather events disrupt supply chains and damage infrastructure, job insecurity becomes a real concern. Middle-class workers may face layoffs, reduced hours, or wage stagnation as their industries struggle to adapt to changing environmental conditions.

4. Housing Market Volatility

Climate change can significantly affect property values. Middle-class homeowners often have a substantial portion of their wealth tied up in their homes. Flooding, sea-level rise, and other climate-related risks can lead to reduced property values, making it challenging for middle-class families to build and protect their assets.

5. Educational Challenges

Climate change can disrupt educational systems through increased extreme weather events, infrastructure damage, health risks, and resource scarcity, leading to school closures, reduced access to education, and overall disruption of learning environments, particularly in vulnerable regions. For middle-class families, this can mean disruptions to their children's education, making it difficult to ensure consistent and high-quality learning experiences.

Conclusion

Environmental concerns and sustainability challenges are intertwined with the lives of the middle class in complex and far-reaching ways. As they strive to make eco-conscious choices while managing budget constraints, the middle class faces a unique set of hurdles that can affect their financial well-being, health, job security, and even their children's education. It's essential to recognize the middle class as a critical demographic in the efforts to address climate change and environmental issues, as they represent a significant portion of the global population.

To address these challenges, governments, businesses, and civil society must work together to create policies and initiatives that make sustainable living more affordable and accessible to the middle class. This can include incentivizing green technologies, expanding public transportation options, and offering financial assistance for energy-efficient home upgrades. Additionally, increasing awareness and education about sustainable living practices can empower the middle class to make informed choices that align with their values and financial constraints.

In a rapidly changing world, where the environment is under constant threat, finding ways to help the middle class overcome the obstacles to sustainable living is not just a matter of social equity but a fundamental step in addressing environmental concerns on a global scale.

Introduction

In today's rapidly evolving economic landscape, the middle class finds itself grappling with an array of challenges. Economic disparities, rising costs of living, and job instability have placed the once-thriving middle class in a precarious position. One of the key aspects of addressing these challenges is the availability and accessibility of social services and safety nets. Safety nets refer to government or social programs and policies designed to provide financial, healthcare, and social assistance to individuals and families who are in need or facing economic hardship, helping to mitigate the impact of poverty and other challenges. In this article, we will explore the vital role of social support systems in the lives of middle-class individuals, and how they navigate government assistance programs, healthcare, and social security to safeguard their well-being.

Access to Social Support: Navigating Government Assistance Programs

The middle class is often depicted as a segment of the population that neither qualifies for significant welfare benefits nor enjoys the safety nets available to the lower-income brackets. This precarious situation necessitates a closer look at how the middle class accesses government assistance programs.

1. The Middle Class Dilemma

The middle class is characterized by its struggle to maintain economic stability. For many, the concept of accessing government assistance might seem distant, reserved for the less fortunate. However, the middle class faces unique challenges that can necessitate government support, such as sudden job loss, medical emergencies, or unexpected financial burdens.

2. The Stigma Surrounding Assistance

One of the challenges middle-class individuals encounter when seeking government assistance is the stigma attached to it. There is often a sense of shame or embarrassment in admitting that one requires help, especially when you belong to a socio-economic group that is expected to be self-sufficient.

3. Navigating the Bureaucracy

Government assistance programs, though vital, can be daunting to navigate. Middle-class individuals may struggle to understand the eligibility criteria, application processes, and the array of available programs. This complexity can deter many from seeking assistance even when they are eligible.

4. The Importance of Information

To address these challenges, there is a growing need for better information dissemination and assistance with navigating government support systems. Non-profit organizations, community centers, and online resources have become essential in guiding middle-class individuals through the process.

Healthcare and Social Security: Discussing the Importance of Safety Nets

Access to quality healthcare and social security is a critical aspect of ensuring the well-being of the middle class. Let's delve into the importance of these safety nets and the challenges middle-class individuals face in securing them.

1. Healthcare and Financial Security

The cost of healthcare in many countries has been on a relentless upward trajectory. Middle-class families can find themselves financially vulnerable in the face of unexpected medical expenses. Health insurance, though essential, can be expensive, and even with coverage, co-pays and deductibles can pose a significant financial burden.

2. The Dilemma of Choice

Middle-class individuals often face the dilemma of choosing between health insurance premiums and other essential expenses. Striking the right balance can be challenging, and many may opt for plans with limited coverage due to budget constraints, leaving them vulnerable to high out-of-pocket costs.

3. Retirement and Social Security

Another crucial aspect of financial security is retirement planning and access to social security benefits. The middle class often struggles to save enough for retirement while balancing day-to-day expenses. Social security can serve as a critical safety net, but its future stability is a growing concern.

To address these challenges, policymakers and employers are increasingly exploring options for making healthcare more affordable for the middle class. Initiatives such as tax-advantaged health savings accounts and employer-sponsored wellness programs aim to provide some relief. Additionally, there is a call for greater transparency in healthcare costs to help middle-class individuals make informed decisions.

Conclusion

The challenges faced by the middle class in accessing social services and safety nets are real and complex. The stigma associated with seeking government assistance, the difficulties in navigating bureaucracy, and the financial vulnerabilities created by healthcare costs are just a few examples of the hurdles this group faces.

Addressing these issues requires a multi-faceted approach. First, there is a need for a shift in societal attitudes to destigmatize government assistance, making it more acceptable for middle-class individuals to seek help when needed. This can be achieved through public awareness campaigns, community support, and education.

Second, simplifying the process of accessing government assistance programs is essential. Governments should work on streamlining application procedures, improving communication, and ensuring that eligibility criteria are clear and easy to understand.

In the realm of healthcare and social security, policymakers must focus on making these services more affordable and accessible to the middle class. This can be achieved through measures like subsidies for health insurance premiums, increasing the minimum wage, and strengthening social security systems.

In the face of evolving economic challenges, a robust and adaptable social safety net is essential to support the middle class. By addressing the unique needs of this group and breaking down the barriers they face in accessing assistance, we can help fortify the middle class and ensure its continued stability and growth. After all, a strong middle class is the cornerstone of a prosperous and equitable society.

Introduction

The issue of inequality and social justice has long been a matter of concern for societies worldwide. In recent years, as societies have evolved and globalized, the middle class has found itself at the intersection of these pressing issues. This article explores the multifaceted dynamics of inequality and social justice, focusing on the middle class's role in addressing these challenges. In particular, we will delve into the wealth gap, examining its implications for society, and discuss the middle class's active role in advocating for social justice.

Wealth Gap: Examining the Implications of Economic Inequality

1. The Middle Class Squeeze

The middle class, often considered the backbone of a nation's economy and society, has faced a unique set of challenges in recent years. One of the most significant challenges is the increasing wealth gap, which has led to a phenomenon known as the "middle class squeeze". This squeeze refers to the situation in which middle-class individuals and families find it increasingly difficult to maintain their standard of living due to rising living costs and stagnant wages.

While the middle class typically enjoys a degree of economic stability, they are not immune to the consequences of economic inequality. In many countries, the wealth gap has expanded, resulting in a middle class that struggles to make ends meet. This not only affects their financial well-being but also their ability to access education, healthcare, and other essential services.

2. Education Disparities

Education is a critical driver of social mobility and is often considered the great equalizer. However, the wealth gap has profound implications for educational disparities. Middle-class families, while not as economically disadvantaged as lower-income families, may still face challenges in providing their children with quality education. In contrast, the wealthy can afford private schools and extracurricular activities that can significantly impact a child's future opportunities.

3. Healthcare Inequities

Access to healthcare is another area where the wealth gap becomes glaringly evident. The middle class often finds itself in a precarious situation regarding healthcare. They may have employer-sponsored health insurance, but the rising costs of premiums, deductibles, and out-of-pocket expenses can lead to financial strain and the potential for medical debt. Meanwhile, those in the upper class have more substantial resources to access the best medical care, leading to stark healthcare inequities.

4. Housing and Homeownership

Homeownership is a traditional hallmark of the middle class. However, economic inequality has made it increasingly difficult for many middle-class individuals and families to purchase homes. Skyrocketing housing prices and stagnant wages create barriers to entry for homeownership. This leads to disparities in wealth accumulation between those who own property and those who do not.

For the middle class, retirement is a vital aspect of economic well-being. However, the wealth gap can threaten the retirement security of middle-class individuals. Stagnant wages, lack of access to employer-sponsored retirement plans, and the rising cost of living make it challenging for the middle class to save adequately for their retirement. This leaves them vulnerable to financial insecurity in their later years, which can have far-reaching consequences.

Advocacy and Activism: The Middle Class's Role in Promoting Social Justice

1. Civic Engagement

Civic engagement refers to the active participation of individuals and communities in the social, political, and cultural life of their society, often involving activities such as voting, volunteering, advocacy, and community involvement to promote positive change and contribute to the well-being of the community.

The middle class, being a significant segment of the population, wields considerable influence in the political arena. Civic engagement is a powerful tool for advocating social justice. Middle-class individuals can participate in elections, join community organizations, and support policies that promote equality and fairness. Their collective voices can shape the political landscape and drive meaningful change.

2. Grassroots Activism

Grassroots activism is a form of political or social activism that begins at the local level, driven by individuals and small groups working to address specific issues or create change within their community, often without significant funding or support from established organizations or institutions.

Social justice movements often gain momentum through grassroots activism. The middle class has a critical role to play in supporting and leading these movements. Whether it's advocating for affordable housing, workers' rights, or environmental sustainability, the middle class can leverage their resources and connections to make a difference in their communities.

3. Charitable Giving

Many middle-class individuals and families engage in charitable giving. While they may not have the financial resources of the wealthy, their contributions, when pooled together, can have a significant impact on various social justice causes. Donations to nonprofits, community organizations, and initiatives that address inequality can be a powerful means of promoting social justice.

4. Advocating for Policy Changes

Policy changes at the local, state, and national levels are fundamental to addressing economic inequality and promoting social justice. The middle class can advocate for policies that support affordable healthcare, education, housing, and workers' rights. Additionally, advocating for progressive tax reforms can help narrow the wealth gap and ensure that the burden of taxation is distributed more equitably.

5. Empowering the Vulnerable

The middle class can play a crucial role in empowering marginalized and vulnerable communities. This can include mentoring, volunteering, and supporting initiatives that provide access to education and job opportunities. By actively working to uplift those who are most affected by economic inequality, the middle class can contribute to a fairer and more just society.

Conclusion

Inequality and social justice are not abstract concepts; they are everyday realities that impact the lives of individuals and families, particularly the middle class. The wealth gap, with its far-reaching implications, places considerable stress on the middle class's economic stability, educational opportunities, healthcare access, homeownership, and retirement security. However, the middle class is not powerless in the face of these challenges.

By actively engaging in advocacy and activism, the middle class can drive meaningful change. Civic engagement, grassroots activism, charitable giving, advocating for policy changes, and empowering vulnerable communities are all avenues through which the middle class can promote social justice. In doing so, they not only improve their own lives but also contribute to a more equitable and fair society.

In the face of the growing wealth gap, the middle class has a unique opportunity to become a force for positive change. By recognizing their role in addressing inequality and promoting social justice, the middle class can navigate the challenges they face and work towards a brighter and more equitable future for all.

Introduction

Political engagement encompasses the various activities and actions that individuals undertake to participate in the political process, including voting in elections, contacting elected officials, attending public meetings, joining political organizations, and engaging in advocacy or activism to influence government policies and decisions.

The middle class is the backbone of any thriving society, serving as the bridge between the economically disadvantaged and the affluent. This socioeconomic group plays a pivotal role in shaping the political landscape of any nation. Political engagement of the middle class is not just a civic duty but a powerful tool to influence government decisions, thus ensuring policies that cater to the needs and aspirations of the majority. In this article, we will delve into the various dimensions of political engagement by the middle class, including representation and policies, as well as grassroots movements that have effectively brought about change. By exploring these aspects, we can understand the challenges faced by the middle class and the potential for them to address these challenges.

Representation and Policies: How the Middle Class Can Influence Government Decisions

1. Voting as a Civic Duty

At the core of political engagement lies the act of voting. The middle class represents a significant portion of the electorate, making their votes invaluable. Casting a ballot in an election is not only a right but a responsibility that empowers citizens to choose leaders who will enact policies that align with their values and priorities. By participating in the electoral process, the middle class can significantly impact government decisions.

2. Advocating for Middle-Class Interests

In addition to voting, active advocacy and participation in the political discourse are essential for the middle class to influence government policies. This includes engaging with elected representatives, attending town hall meetings, and organizing grassroots campaigns. Through these efforts, middle-class individuals and groups can articulate their needs and concerns, ensuring that the government takes their interests into account when formulating policies.

3. Lobbying and Interest Groups

The middle class can further their influence by forming or joining interest groups and lobbying organizations. These groups pool resources, knowledge, and expertise to effectively advocate for policies that benefit the middle class. They work closely with lawmakers and government officials to ensure that the concerns of this socioeconomic group are heard and addressed.

4. Running for Office

Another powerful way to influence government decisions is by having middle-class individuals run for political office. When middle-class candidates become part of the decision-making process, they bring a unique perspective and firsthand experience of the challenges faced by their constituents. This can lead to the creation of policies that better serve the middle class.

In some cases, the middle class may need to support and promote political reforms that make the system more democratic and responsive to their needs. This might include advocating for campaign finance reform, promoting transparency in government, and pushing for electoral system improvements.

Grassroots Movements: Examples of Middle-Class-Led Initiatives for Change

1. Civil Rights Movement

One of the most iconic examples of grassroots movements led by the middle class is the Civil Rights Movement in the United States during the 1950s and 1960s. The middle class, both Black and White, played a pivotal role in advocating for racial equality and social justice. Through nonviolent protests, civil disobedience, and organized actions, they pushed for legal and policy changes that eventually led to the end of segregation and the protection of civil rights for all.

2. Environmental Activism

Environmental concerns have been a driving force for many middle-class-led movements. Groups like Greenpeace, Sierra Club, and Extinction Rebellion have garnered widespread support and have influenced government policies on climate change, pollution control, and conservation efforts. The middle class has been instrumental in raising awareness and advocating for sustainable policies.

3. Women's Rights Movement

The women's rights movement refers to a social and political campaign that advocates for the equal rights and opportunities of women, addressing issues such as suffrage, reproductive rights, workplace equality, and gender discrimination. It has evolved over time, with different waves and phases of activism, all aiming to advance women's rights and gender equality.

The women's rights movement is another example of middle-class-led activism that has shaped government policies. Women from the middle class and their allies fought for equal rights, leading to legal reforms that include voting rights, reproductive rights, and workplace equality. Their efforts have significantly influenced government decisions on gender-related issues.

4. Labor Movements

Labor movements are organized efforts by workers to collectively advocate for their rights and interests, typically with the goal of improving working conditions, wages, and other labor-related issues. These movements often involve labor unions and various forms of collective action, including strikes and negotiations with employers.

Throughout history, the middle class has also been at the forefront of labor movements. Organizations like labor unions and worker advocacy groups have played a critical role in advocating for workers' rights, fair wages, and workplace safety. Their collective actions have led to government policies that protect the interests of the working class and the middle class.

In many countries, middle-class parents have organized to advocate for improvements in the education system. They have pushed for better school funding, improved curricula, and enhanced teacher training. These movements have not only led to better educational opportunities for their own children but have also influenced government decisions on education policy.

Conclusion

The challenges faced by the middle class are diverse and significant, including economic stability, access to quality education, healthcare, affordable housing, and more. To address these challenges and ensure that government decisions align with the interests of the middle class, political engagement is essential.

The middle class can influence government decisions by actively participating in the democratic process, advocating for their interests, and supporting policies and reforms that benefit their socioeconomic group. By voting, engaging with elected representatives, forming interest groups, running for office, and advocating for political reforms, the middle class can make their voices heard and shape government policies to better reflect their needs and aspirations.

Furthermore, grassroots movements led by the middle class have a rich history of effecting change on a larger scale. From the civil rights movement to environmental activism, these movements have not only raised awareness but also influenced government decisions on important social, economic, and environmental issues.

In the challenges of the middle class, political engagement emerges as a powerful tool for progress and change. It is a means by which the middle class can assert its collective voice, shape the direction of the nation, and create a better future for themselves and their fellow citizens. Through active participation and advocacy, the middle class can ensure that government decisions are not only representative but also responsive to their needs, ultimately leading to a more equitable and prosperous society.

Introduction

The middle class, often seen as the backbone of society, faces its own set of unique challenges, and one of the most significant among these is the issue of mental health and well-being. In an era marked by technological advancements, high work demands, and the relentless pursuit of material success, the mental health of the middle class often takes a backseat. This article delves into the various aspects of mental health within the middle class, focusing on stress, burnout, stigma, and the barriers to treatment. It seeks to shed light on the often-overlooked mental health struggles of this demographic, ultimately advocating for the importance of prioritizing one's psychological well-being.

Stress and Burnout: Addressing the Psychological Toll of Modern Middle-Class Life

1. The Perils of the Modern Middle-Class Lifestyle

The middle class typically finds itself sandwiched between the struggles of the lower class and the pressures of the upper class. While this demographic may not contend with extreme poverty or the stress of maintaining extravagant lifestyles, it often grapples with its own set of difficulties. The demands of the modern middle-class lifestyle are relentless, as individuals strive to balance work, family, and personal ambitions. This constant juggling act can give rise to chronic stress, which, if left unaddressed, can lead to burnout.

Stress has become a pervasive issue in middle-class life. The 9-to-5 job, often accompanied by long commutes and the expectation to be perpetually connected to work through technology, can take a significant toll on one's mental health. Additionally, the pressure to provide a comfortable lifestyle for one's family, the desire to climb the corporate ladder, and the fear of economic instability contribute to stress. Over time, this stress can manifest in physical symptoms, such as sleep disturbances, headaches, and digestive issues.

3. The Consequences of Burnout

When stress remains unaddressed, it can escalate into burnout, a state of physical, emotional, and mental exhaustion. Burnout can manifest as a complete loss of motivation, feelings of cynicism, and a decline in productivity. The consequences of burnout are far-reaching, affecting not only the individual's personal well-being but also their relationships and overall quality of life. It can lead to absenteeism at work, reduced job satisfaction, and even long-term health issues.

Seeking Help: Overcoming Mental Health Stigma and Barriers to Treatment

1. The Stigma Surrounding Mental Health

In the middle-class milieu, seeking help for mental health issues often carries a significant stigma. There's a pervasive notion that middle-class individuals should be able to cope with their problems independently, as acknowledging mental health concerns can be seen as a sign of weakness. This stigma contributes to a culture of silence around mental health, discouraging individuals from seeking the support they need.

2. Barriers to Treatment

Even when individuals are willing to seek help, barriers to accessing mental health treatment can be formidable. The cost of therapy and medications can be prohibitive for many middle-class families, especially those without comprehensive health insurance. Additionally, long wait times for mental health services and a shortage of mental health professionals in some regions can create further obstacles.

3. The Importance of Awareness and Education

To combat the stigma surrounding mental health in the middle class, raising awareness and promoting education is crucial. Schools, workplaces, and communities need to foster open dialogues about mental health, normalizing discussions about stress, anxiety, and depression. Mental health education can empower individuals to recognize the signs of distress in themselves and others, reducing the stigma and encouraging timely intervention.

4. Advocating for Accessible Treatment

Addressing barriers to treatment involves advocating for accessible mental health services. Government policies, employers, and healthcare providers can play a pivotal role in making mental health services affordable and available. Initiatives such as employee assistance programs (EAPs) and telehealth options have the potential to bridge the gap between middle-class individuals and much-needed mental health support.

Conclusion

The challenges of the middle class extend beyond the economic sphere. The pressures of modern middle-class life can have a profound impact on mental health and well-being. Stress and burnout have become alarmingly common, yet are often ignored or underestimated. Overcoming these challenges necessitates a two-fold approach: addressing the psychological toll of middle-class life and breaking down the stigma and barriers that surround mental health treatment.

To safeguard the mental health of the middle class, it is essential to foster awareness, provide education, and promote open discussions about mental well-being. Empowering individuals to seek help without shame is paramount, as is making treatment accessible and affordable. By acknowledging the unique struggles of the middle class and working collectively to support their mental health, society can help ensure a happier, healthier, and more productive middle class that thrives, rather than merely survives, in the demanding landscape of modern life.

Introduction

The middle class has long been regarded as the backbone of any thriving society, serving as a stabilizing force in economies and communities worldwide. However, the challenges faced by the middle class are evolving rapidly in the 21st century. In this article, we will explore the future prospects of the middle class, taking into account the ever-changing landscape of employment, necessary policy adaptations, and the crucial role of education. As we delve into the complexities of these issues, it becomes evident that the middle class, traditionally seen as the bedrock of societal stability, is at a critical juncture that requires innovative thinking and proactive measures.

Technology and Work: Preparing for the Changing Landscape of Employment

1. Automation and Job Displacement

The advent of automation and artificial intelligence technologies has significantly impacted the job market. While these technologies have the potential to increase productivity and efficiency, they also pose a significant threat to traditional middle-class jobs. Routine, repetitive tasks are increasingly being automated, leaving workers in those roles at risk of displacement. The middle class, traditionally reliant on these jobs, faces the challenge of adapting to this new reality.

To prepare for this changing landscape, it's essential that the middle class invests in education and training to acquire skills that are less susceptible to automation. This may mean transitioning from manual labor to jobs that require creativity, complex problem-solving, and interpersonal skills. Lifelong learning is becoming a necessity, with workers needing to continually update their skill sets to remain relevant in the job market.

2. Gig Economy and Income Instability

The gig economy, characterized by short-term contracts and freelance work, is on the rise. While it offers flexibility, it also comes with income instability and a lack of traditional benefits like healthcare and retirement plans. Many middle-class workers are turning to gig work to make ends meet, but this often means living paycheck to paycheck with little job security.

To address this issue, policymakers should explore ways to provide gig workers with essential benefits and protections. Portable benefits, such as healthcare plans that individuals can carry with them between jobs, can offer a solution. Additionally, creating a safety net for gig workers, akin to traditional unemployment benefits, can help alleviate the financial uncertainties that come with gig employment.

3. Globalization and Outsourcing

Globalization has opened up new markets and opportunities, but it has also led to the outsourcing of jobs to countries with lower labor costs. This has had a significant impact on the middle class, particularly in industries like manufacturing. As companies seek cost-effective solutions, middle-class workers often bear the brunt of job losses.

One way to address this challenge is to encourage domestic job growth through incentives for companies that keep jobs onshore. Policies that promote reshoring and support the growth of local industries can help create new opportunities for the middle class. Additionally, fostering an environment that encourages entrepreneurship and small business growth can provide new avenues for middle-class workers to thrive in an evolving global economy.

Policy Recommendations: Proposing Changes to Support the Middle Class in the Future

1. Investment in Education

One of the fundamental ways to support the middle class in the future is by investing in education. As automation and technological advancements continue to reshape the job market, individuals need to acquire skills that are in demand. This necessitates a robust and flexible education system that promotes lifelong learning.

Policymakers should consider measures like increasing funding for vocational and technical education, making higher education more affordable, and providing retraining opportunities for displaced workers. Furthermore, promoting STEM (Science, Technology, Engineering, and Mathematics) education can prepare individuals for the jobs of the future, ensuring they remain competitive in a rapidly changing world.

2. Social Safety Nets

To address the challenges of income instability in the gig economy, there is a need for a modernized social safety net. Policies should be reevaluated to accommodate the changing nature of work, and benefits such as healthcare, retirement savings, and unemployment insurance should be made more portable, allowing workers to maintain these benefits even as they switch jobs or engage in gig work.

A universal basic income (UBI) is another concept worth exploring, as it could provide a financial safety net for all citizens, helping to alleviate poverty and income inequality. UBI is a social welfare policy in which the government provides all citizens or residents with a regular, unconditional sum of money, typically on a monthly basis, to cover basic living expenses, regardless of their employment status or income level. By providing a guaranteed income, it would reduce the anxiety associated with job loss and income fluctuations, allowing the middle class to invest in their future with more confidence.

3. Tax Reforms

Tax policies should be reformed to ensure that the burden of supporting the middle class is distributed fairly. Progressive taxation that places a heavier burden on the wealthy can be a way to fund essential social programs while reducing the financial strain on the middle class.

In addition, policymakers should consider ways to incentivize saving and wealth-building among middle-class families. This may include tax deductions for retirement savings, homeownership, and education expenses. By reducing the financial barriers to these essential life goals, the middle class can build economic stability for the future.

4. Worker Protections

Worker protections need to be extended and adapted to the changing workforce. As more individuals engage in gig work and non-traditional employment, they should still enjoy the same rights and protections as traditional employees. This includes access to healthcare, retirement benefits, and legal recourse for labor violations.

Moreover, policies should be put in place to address wage stagnation and ensure that the middle class can benefit from economic growth. Raising the minimum wage and indexing it to inflation is one way to help workers earn a fair wage that keeps up with the cost of living.

Conclusion

The challenges faced by the middle class are in a state of constant flux, driven by technological advancements, shifts in the job market, and evolving economic realities. To secure a prosperous future for the middle class, it is essential to take proactive measures. This includes adapting to changing employment landscapes by investing in education and retraining, establishing a modernized social safety net, reforming tax policies, and extending worker protections.

While the challenges are significant, so too are the opportunities. By embracing innovation, cultivating adaptability, and fostering a sense of economic security, the middle class can not only weather the storms of change but also thrive in the future. Policymakers, educators, and society at large must come together to build a stronger, more resilient middle class that continues to be the cornerstone of thriving societies worldwide. In doing so, we ensure a brighter and more stable future for all.

"Challenges of the Middle Class" delves into the intricate web of struggles, aspirations, and resilience that defines the modern middle class. This comprehensive exploration, spanning sixteen thought-provoking chapters, elucidates the multifaceted issues faced by this socio-economic group. From economic pressures, educational dilemmas, and healthcare concerns to housing struggles, family-work balance, and retirement uncertainties, this book offers an in-depth analysis of the challenges middle-class individuals grapple with daily.

Moreover, it examines social mobility, financial management, technological disruption, environmental concerns, and the vital role of social services. It further delves into the intricate landscape of inequality and social justice, political engagement, mental health, and the prospects for a future marked by technological change and policy evolution. A must-read for anyone seeking a profound understanding of the struggles and potential solutions for the middle class in the contemporary world.

ABOUT THE AUTHOR

Mr. C. P. Kumar is a retired Scientist 'G' from National Institute of Hydrology, Roorkee, Uttarakhand, India. He is also a Reiki Healer and Chakra Balancing practitioner (with pendulum dowsing) and offers Emotional Freedom Technique (EFT) to help individuals with emotional issues. Mr. Kumar has authored many books on technical, spiritual, and social topics.

For further details, you may visit his webpage
https://www.angelfire.com/nh/cpkumar/virgo.html